This uplifting collection of poems,
short stories, and relevant scripture verses
invites readers on a

Heartfelt Journey of
Hope, Faith and Love

Every mile, every loss,
Leads us deeper into the cross,
Through the dark, through the dawn,
We are held, We are not alone.

Invited to a glorious world yet unseen,
To wear pure linen of righteousness,
With joy and excitement,
Woven not by hands, but by mercy.

He stood before the gates,
a glorious light pouring through.
A voice called out to him with love,
"Welcome home, my child."

†

For here we have no lasting city,
but we seek the city that is to come.
Hebrews 13:14 (ESV)

ABE KOSH

SEED TO A FLAME

FROM THE SEED OF FAITH TO A RISING FLAME OF DIVINE LOVE

ABE KOSH

PREFACE

Seed to a Flame was born from a deep stirring in my heart—a desire to express the quiet and profound beauty of a life given over to God. Where other forms of communication often felt inadequate to convey what I longed to share, writing became the means through which I could give shape to those truths.

By God's grace, my education and experience in law, business, and technology, together with a life lived across continents and cultures, have enabled me to translate decades of reflection and experience into poems and short stories. These writings are not merely literary efforts, but humble offerings shaped by the many places I have lived, the many people I have encountered, and the many ways I have witnessed God's hand at work. Having grown up in India, I witnessed hardship closely and experienced my own share of trials. Later, through life in other countries and through the education I was blessed to receive, I came to see more deeply the steadfastness of God's providence toward those who believe, obey, and surrender to Him.

Over the years, I have sought to understand the insights of philosophers, jurists, and theologians in practical, simple ways, first for my own growth and then to communicate and share them. The poems and short stories in this book are the fruit of that effort. They arise from a life shaped by faith, discipline, learning, and experience across many fields. Yet, all of them point toward one enduring truth: that God remains present, faithful, and beautiful in the daily journey of a Christian life.

My aim in these pages is simple: to present, in clear and accessible terms, the truth, goodness, and beauty of God as experienced in the life of a Christian. This beauty exists not apart from struggle, sorrow, or the brokenness of the world, but often shines most clearly through them.

The twelve poems in this book, which have also been adapted as song lyrics and made available on major streaming platforms, are shared alongside the short stories with the prayer that, together, they may find a place in receptive, loving hearts. Above all, I pray that they may serve the glory of God.

May these pages encourage reflection, awaken hope, and kindle devotion so that what begins as a seed in the heart may, by God's grace, grow into a flame.

Uponthefinalmile.com

AUTHOR'S NOTE

I offer my deepest gratitude to my beloved wife, my precious daughter, my siblings, and the many cherished family members and dear friends who have supported, encouraged, and uplifted me throughout my life. Their love, patience, and steadfast presence have been among my greatest blessings, and I carry that gratitude with me every day.

I thank God for each of them, and it is my sincere prayer that He grants them His very best: abundant joy, peace, good health, and grace; in every season of their lives, as well as to the communities to which they belong and contribute.

To my beloved late parents, thank you for your endless love, sacrifices, and guidance, which continue to live in my heart and shape every page of this book.

I am also grateful to call Texas my current home, where I am surrounded by a beautiful, peaceful, and loving community that has enriched my life in countless ways.

With a thankful heart, I dedicate these words in honor of all who have walked beside me with love and faith.

CONTENTS

PART XII

PART I

HOPE IS NOT LOST

Desperate by the lake,
A torturous soul,
A fish out of fresh water,
From a pond to a saline ocean.
Hope is not lost,
Lifting hands in prayer,
A dive into God's mercy,
Where the waves can't break trust.
Seeking fervently,
Desiring truth,
Yielding to Spirit's gracious guidance,
Joy infused, burden becomes light.
The fruit of the Holy Spirit,
Internalized,
Once broken, now is beauty,
What was burden, now a blessing,
Passion for the Savior,
Outshines all struggles.
Mirroring Christ's selfless love,
Joy and glory lived in loving sacrifice,
Where every act of love for God,
Ultimately, works for the best.

Hope is not Lost-Music

The lake was calm early in the morning, with a peaceful sunrise, golden light illuminating the sky and reflecting on the water.

In the distance, the city rose, its skyscrapers shining with light, their glass exteriors flashing like distant flames. They stood tall, full of ambition and pride. But here, at the lake's edge, there was stillness.

Asher stood alone by the lake.

The wind gently pressed against his untucked shirt, carrying the foul smell of sewage from nearby industrial waste and garbage dumps. The freshwater lake flowed into the river and out to the Indian Ocean. He had grown up near small ponds and paddy fields miles away—still, gentle, and predictable. Life had once been simple.

Now it felt like an ocean.

"This is torture," he muttered to himself, watching ripples disturb his reflection. "A fish out of fresh water."

The city in the distance was a symbol of opportunity and success. But managing endless sales stress and crowded trains made him feel drained, like a fish gasping for air on a dock, lungs made for something else. From pond to a saline ocean, the transition had stung. He had not been ready for the salt and the wounds.

For months, he carried this weight quietly, smiling at work, nodding in meetings, laughter never quite reaching his eyes. Despite his weekend escapism, he was broke and exhausted. As the skyscrapers grew taller, his spirit sank lower.

Today, the burden felt especially heavy.

He stepped closer to the lake and looked across its broad surface. The water was calm despite the hum of the city. It was as if the lake refused to reflect the chaos ahead. Instead, it held the sky.

Hope is not lost.

Those words floated in his mind like something from childhood, a verse, a prayer, a whisper from long ago. He had nearly forgotten how to pray.

Slowly, Asher raised his hands.

There, by the water, with distant skyscrapers as silent witnesses, he closed his eyes.

"God," he breathed.

No rehearsed speech. No eloquent confession. A cry, heavy with need.

A feeling of plunging into depths he had resisted, a dive into God's mercy. He had tried to cope with anxiety through pride and strength, determined to prove he could excel on his own. But the tide had been too strong.

Now he let himself sink, not into despair but into trust.

As the wind brushed his unshaven face, he allowed the water to embrace him instead of fighting it. He decided to yield rather than resist. Seeking earnestly, craving truth more than approval or applause.

"Please show me what is real," he pleaded. "Show me my identity in You."

Silence responded, but not emptiness. It was the quiet that assured stability.

A warm feeling of peace rested on him, the joy of knowing that he is seen, known, and loved. An assurance amidst tall towers and restless ambition, and he felt confident.

"Trust in the Lord and be led by His Spirit."

The phrase came gently, and with it a shift, a burden loosening its grip. His uncertainties still real. But something inside had changed.

He lowered his hands and opened his eyes.

The lake now reflected the sun's golden light, sparkling beautifully on the surface. The skyscrapers no longer felt like pressure; they were just buildings, tools, places where life unfolded. They had no power over his worth or identity.

He realized he had been seeking love, joy, and peace in the skyline when they had always been waiting within him; they are deeply rooted gifts to receive.

Nearby, he picked up an abandoned folding chair, straightened it, and sat down. He appreciated its beauty despite its worn appearance. *When grace enters the heart, failures fade, confidence flows, and the surrounding environment is appreciated with gratitude.* He was surprised that such a thought would come to him; he chuckled.

He wondered if, had the ocean not overwhelmed him, he would ever have learned to float.

A jogger ran in the distance, a couple showed affection near the path, and a child pointed excitedly at the swimming ducklings following the mother across the lake. Life continued, remarkable and sacred.

Asher felt something new rise within him, not the frantic urge to conquer the skyline, but a passion for the Savior who met him beside the lake. A quiet fire that outshined all struggles.

Recalling scripture, he thought of small acts of love: volunteering at local charities, encouraging coworkers, and giving without expecting recognition. Living in loving sacrifice, not as loss but as triumph.

Asher experienced a revival, a breath of fresh life, a conviction that the skyscrapers are part of a larger canvas with the lake softening the edges.

He was no longer a fish gasping on the dock. He was learning the currents, understanding that grace sustains even in salt water.

Learning that the One who formed the pond also commands the sea.

The lake remained calm as he walked away, its surface still reflecting the towers in quiet splendor.

Behind him, the city basked in morning sunlight.

Within him, something brighter.

Isaiah 40:31 (NIV)

but those who hope in the Lord
will renew their strength.
They will soar on wings like eagles;
they will run and not grow weary,
they will walk and not be faint.

PART II

SEEKING GRACE

A Swan in distress from swallowing pain,
Drifted alone on a wind-swept plain.
Its wings hung low, its song a sigh,
A tearful plea beneath the sky.
Released a feather, soft and white,
Dancing through the air,
In trembling flight.
A beacon sent in the hush of grief,
A calling out, a cry for relief.
Oh, let it capture heaven's gaze,
This floating feather's fragile praise.
Its beauty born from a silent plea,
To the sacred heart,
Of the one who is love.
Missionaries, devoted hearts in Christ,
Moved by grace, took flight, took part,
Descending swiftly on wings of care,
To lift the swan from dark despair.
So pain may pass, and light remains,
Where once there dwelled,
Such swallowing pain,
Peace may glide on waters wide,
With healing feathers at its side.

Seeking Grace-Music

In a quiet valley where the winds wandered freely across endless plains, there lived a swan known among the creatures of the water as Aurelia, the Silent Singer.

Once, Aurelia's voice had been the most beautiful sound on the lake. At dawn, she would glide across silver waters, her song rising with the mist like a hymn of gratitude to the heavens. The reeds swayed when she sang, and even the restless winds paused to listen.

But one winter, everything changed.

A bitter storm had swept across the valley, scattering the waters and chilling the earth. During those harsh days, Aurelia swallowed more than the cold. She swallowed sorrow—loss, loneliness, and a quiet pain she could not release. It settled deep within her heart like a stone beneath the water's surface.

As spring returned, the lake came alive again, but Aurelia did not. She drifted away from the others, carried by the winds onto a lonely plain where the grasses bent beneath the sky. Her once-proud wings hung low at her sides, and when she tried to sing, only a trembling sigh escaped.

The heavens seemed wide and silent above her.

One evening, as twilight painted the sky fading pink, Aurelia felt the weight in her heart grow too heavy to bear alone. With a gentle movement of her wing, she released a single feather.

It was soft and white as fresh snow.

The feather caught the evening breeze and rose into the air. It danced and trembled as it traveled upward, drifting beyond the quiet plain, beyond the restless winds, as though it carried a message written in silence.

It was not merely a feather.

It was a prayer.

Higher and higher it floated, until it seemed to reach the listening heavens themselves. And though the earth below could not see it, the sacred heart of Love heard the fragile plea carried in that drifting white feather.

Far away, in places where faith moved quietly through human hearts, there were people who listened to such whispers.

They were missionaries, souls devoted to Christ, men and women who believed that even the smallest cry of suffering was never lost in the vastness of the world. When grace stirred within them, they moved without hesitation.

And grace did stir.

As if guided by unseen wings, they journeyed across lands and waters until they reached the lonely plain where Aurelia wandered in sorrow. Their presence was gentle, their hearts filled not with judgment but with care.

They did not force the swan to rise.

Instead, they knelt beside her stillness.

They tended to her with patience, spoke words of hope like warm light in winter, and reminded the weary swan that pain, no matter how deeply swallowed, was never meant to be carried alone.

Slowly, the stone within Aurelia's heart began to dissolve.

The winds softened. The sky seemed brighter. And one morning, when the sun spilled gold across the lake, Aurelia felt strength return to her wings.

She stepped into the water once more.

This time, when she sang, the sound was different. It carried the memory of sorrow, but also the miracle of healing. The lake shimmered with the echo of it.

Pain had passed.

Light remained.

And wherever Aurelia glided across the waters, white feathers sometimes drifted beside her, not as cries of despair, but as quiet reminders that even the smallest prayer can rise to heaven, and God's Love will always prevail.

Psalm 34:17-18

The righteous cry out,
and the Lord hears them;
he delivers them from
all their troubles.
The Lord is close
to the brokenhearted
and saves those
who are crushed in spirit.

PART III

GARDEN OF DIVINE LIGHT

A dream, seeking salvation—
Kneeling,
Before the ultimate high priest,
In a garden of divine light,
Shining over worship.
Amidst reverent blaze roses,
Where bluebirds gather,
For earnest play,
Petals unfold like whispered prayer,
Frankincense fragrance warms the air,
Angels keep vigil,
The cherished vulnerable are saved,
In this place of holy grace.
Every heart finds peace and space.

Garden of Divine Light-Music

In the quiet hours before dawn, when the world still trembled between darkness and light, a dream entered the heart of a weary traveler.

The traveler had wandered far, though years filled with noise, doubt, and longing. The road behind was heavy with questions, and the path ahead seemed lost in mist. Yet on this night, sleep opened a gate, and through it, the traveler stepped into a garden unlike any known on earth.

The air shimmered with a gentle, vibrant glow. It was not the harsh brilliance of the sun but a divine light that seemed to breathe—soft, patient, and endlessly kind. At the center of the garden stood the ultimate high priest, whose majestic presence radiated pure love, gravity, and peace.

The traveler instinctively knelt.

Around him, blaze roses burned with deep crimson petals, glowing as if they held small flames of reverence. Yet their fire was tender, like devotion itself. Between the roses, bluebirds fluttered playfully, darting through the light as if joy were their only language.

Their songs filled the garden.

Petals unfurled slowly across the branches, opening like whispered prayers rising from the earth. With each bloom, the fragrance of frankincense drifted through the air—warm, sacred, and ancient. It wrapped the garden in a quiet hush that felt like being embraced.

High above, angels kept vigil.

They did not speak or move with spectacle. They watched with calm, luminous eyes, guardians of a peace too precious to disturb. Their wings flashed in the garden's light, like clouds touched by dawn.

The traveler observed others there, people kneeling, carrying burdens much like his own. Some were wounded, frightened, or fragile in spirit. Yet here, beneath the watch of the angels and the steady presence of the ultimate high priest, something remarkable happened.

No one was turned away.

The vulnerable were gathered close. The lost were seen. The

broken were not judged but welcomed as if they had always belonged. One by one, their fears softened, like frost melting beneath morning light.

The traveler felt free and at peace.

For years, his heart had been tight with worry and regret. But in this holy garden, surrounded by roses, birds singing, and the quiet breath of incense, the weight began to fall away.

Peace did not arrive suddenly; it unfolded like petals.

The traveler bowed his head, and for the first time in a long while, he did not ask for answers. He rested in the grace that filled the garden, a grace large enough for every sorrow and hope.

Here, no heart was heavy or fragile.

In this place of holy grace, every heart found peace and space.

And when the traveler finally woke, the garden was gone, but its light remained,

quietly blooming within him.

Hebrews 4:14-16 (NIV)

Therefore, since we have a great high priest who has ascended into heaven, Jesus the Son of God, let us hold firmly to the faith we profess. For we do not have a high priest who is unable to empathize with our weaknesses, but we have one who has been tempted in every way, just as we are—yet he did not sin. Let us then approach God's throne of grace with confidence, so that we may receive mercy and find grace to help us in our time of need.

PART IV

FROM DEATH TO LIFE

Clothed in glittering lies,
Forms of idolatry corrupt desires,
Distort the way.
Through deception's ancient whisper,
Distractions lure the soul astray.
With laser focus fixed on truth,
Scripture's light sets captives free.
Rejoice! Glorious victory,
In Christ's sacrificial love!
Distractions die, souls ascend,
Toward unseen beauty,
Boundless grace.
Love poured out despite our failures,
The gift of redemption,
Offered to everyone.
God's glory wraps the world in light,
Passed from death to life,
To all who believe!

From Death to Life-Music

In the town of Gamala, every street sparkled.

Neon signs lit the buildings in color. Market stalls overflowed with jewels, perfumes, and clever little devices that promised instant happiness. Above every doorway, smiling faces drew crowds with clever slogans: "This will satisfy you." "This will complete you." "You deserve this."

And the people believed them.

Among them walked a woman named Mara, who had spent years chasing the glitter. She wore fine clothes, spoke polished words, and filled every moment with worldly passions. Yet at night, when the lights dimmed, and the crowds went home, she felt hollow, as if her soul had wandered somewhere she could not follow.

One evening, deep in the heart of the town, Mara heard a whisper behind the music and laughter.

It was old, smooth, and familiar.

"You need only one more thing."

So she turned and eagerly sought the source.

As she crossed a narrow alley, she noticed something strange: a small door stood open between two fancy shops. Inside, there was no music, no perfume, no dazzling display. Only a single lamp burned beside a worn wooden table, and on it lay an open book.

Drawn by a hunger she could not name, Mara stepped inside.

An older man sat near the lamp, reading. He looked up and smiled, not with the thin smile of a merchant, but with the warmth of someone who had already found treasure.

"You look tired, are you looking for something?" he asked.

Mara almost laughed. "I have everything I wanted."

The older man nodded toward the book. "Then why are you still searching?"

She had no answer.

He turned the pages and began to read aloud. The words were unlike the town's shining promises. They did not flatter her. They pierced her. They named the idols she had dressed in beauty. They uncovered the lies she had loved. Yet with every word, another thing happened too: the heaviness inside her began to shrink, as though chains she had worn so long were falling to the floor.

"This light," the old man said gently, "does not deceive. It shows the wound, but it also reveals the Healer."

Mara listened as he told her of Christ; of love poured out for the undeserving, of mercy stronger than failure, of the Holy One who entered death itself to lead captives into life. Not a love to be bought. Not a glory made of mirrors. A sacrificial love. A redeeming love. A victorious love.

And for the first time, Mara saw the glittering town clearly.

Its brilliance was only a borrowed sparkle. Its promises were cages painted to look like crowns. The ancient whisper behind it all had never wanted to fill her soul, only to keep it wandering.

She fell to her knees beside the table, weeping; not only repenting for what she had chased, but for the wonder that she, too, was invited. That redemption was not for the flawless, but for the lost; not for a chosen few, but for everyone who would believe.

Outside, the town still blazed. But inside that humble room, a brighter light rose.

When Mara stepped back into the street, the signs still flashed and the merchants still called, but their voices had lost their power. The glitter no longer ruled her gaze. Her heart had found the true, ultimate center.

She walked on, not upward by ladder or throne, but inward and higher all at once; toward an unseen beauty, toward boundless grace.

And as dawn broke over Gamala, the glitter of the town faded before the morning sun.

People looked up from their distractions and saw Mara's face, peaceful and radiant. Some mocked. Some turned away. But others, weary like she had been, followed her to the little open door.

There, the lamp still burned, and the word of God is living and active.

And there, beneath the mercy of Christ, souls passed from death to life, the glory of God wrapping the world in grace.

Psalm 119:105 (ESV)

Your word is a lamp to my feet
and a light to my path.

PART V

THE TRUE ROAD HOME

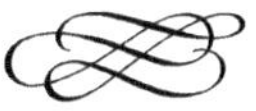

Awakened by Gospel's light,
And cheered by hymns of peace,
We proclaim,
In the Spirit's sacred flame,
And grow in repentance,
And selfless love.
We learn love,
Beyond the bounds of time,
Through joy and piercing pain.
We live by the faithful Word,
The rock of Truth,
Our everlasting strength.
The call goes out, so strong, so clear:
Come seek,
The heavenly joy meant for all.
Immerse yourself, be cleansed,
Be born anew, in the pool,
Where living waters flow through.
Not for the crowd, not for the praise,
But for the love that lights our days.
One heart, one faith,
One song we sing:
The risen Jesus, our hope, our King.
Washed in grace, we rise and go,
Led by the Spirit—
We follow, we flourish.
This is the road, not easy, but true,
The path of peace for me and you.

The True Road Home-Music

On a Sunday morning, Charles woke up to the light that had already filled the room, softly bright and gently spilling across the blanket, and the white cast that supported his leg, still as stone. For a moment, he did not move. He listened. Beyond the open crack of the window, from somewhere down the street and across the small row of sycamores, the Church bells gave a single bright peal, followed by the faint rising of voices, hymns carried thin and tender through the spring air.

He lay in his narrow bed, feeling the ache that had become his first companion each morning. It was not the wild pain of the hospital days, nor the sharp, blazing sensation that had torn through him after the accident. Instead, it was quieter now, deeper, a piercing reminder. It lived in the bone, in the muscle, in the long hours still to come before he could walk without fear. Some mornings, it made him bitter; other mornings, it made him so tired he wept.

But this morning, the singing reached him first. He couldn't make out every word, only the shapes—a lift, a surrender, a certainty. They came to him as if through water, yet were clear enough to steady something in him that had been drifting for weeks. He watched the dust swirl in the sunlight and thought how strange it was that grace could arrive so lightly: in a bell, in a choir he could barely hear, on a Sunday morning he hadn't chosen and couldn't fully join yet. He had once believed strength meant movement, work, and the power to carry on and endure without asking for help. But injury had stripped those notions from him. It had lowered him into this bed and taught him the helplessness of being washed, fed, and lifted by others. In the long, humiliating days, something in him had broken open beside the body. Pride, perhaps. Or the illusion that love could be earned through usefulness.

Again, the voices floated toward him. Not for the crowd, he thought suddenly, not for praise. The words were not spoken aloud, but they moved through him with the quiet authority of truth. Not for the crowd, not for praise, but for love. For the mother who changed the water pitcher each evening and never mentioned her own tiredness. For the friend who sat awkwardly by the bed and talked about ordinary things until they both forgot to be embarrassed. For the old pastor who had come once, placed a hand on his shoulder, and said only, "Healing is not always the body first."

He turned his head toward the window. The sky was pale blue, rinsed clean. Somewhere beyond his sight, the congregation was standing now, singing with one heart, one faith, one song. He pictured their open hymnals, the worn wood pews, the colored light slipping through stained glass. And though he remained in bed, in pain, bound by weakness, he did not feel outside of it. The sound reached him as a call; strong, clear, meant even for him.

Come.

Not 'come' when you are whole. Not come until you can stand straight, walk unassisted, and return to being admired for your strength. Just come.

He closed his eyes again, not to sleep, but to receive the morning. Beneath the ache in his body, there was now another sensation: small but alive—hope. Not the loud hope of sudden miracles, but the patient kind, the kind that rises bathed in grace and learns, slowly, to begin again.

The hymn floated on. He breathed with it.

He knew this road wouldn't be easy. Recovery would demand more than endurance. It would require repentance for the hardness he had mistaken for courage. It would ask for trust. It would require humility to be loved. Yet, in the warm Gospel light of that Sunday, with the Church nearby enough to hear, and heaven appearing, for one quiet hour, not far at all, the road ahead no longer seemed empty.

It looked real, and he believed!

And there, in his bed, while bells faded and the last hymn trembled in the air, the man smiled to himself—because at last he understood that even through piercing pain, he was being led somewhere holy, somewhere gentle, and somewhere joyful.

Toward peace.

Toward life.

Toward the living waters, already flowing.

Galatians 5:25 (NIV)

Since we live by the Spirit,
let us keep in step with the Spirit.

PART VI

UPON THE FINAL MILE

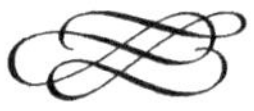

Upon the Final Mile,
Set aside all broken ways,
Grudges we've carried for days,
Kneeling before God's grace,
Carve out iniquities,
For it is written,
"Be holy, because I am holy."
From the rhythms of life, rise up,
Ready to battle disruptions,
Rise up, like the purple perennials,
From among the thorns and thistles.
Upon the final mile,
Find the anointed beauty,
Of God's redemptive purpose,
Even through suffering,
To choose life, not death.
A canvas of assurance unfolded,
Beautifully painted,
A mysterious citadel,
Flashing exquisite colors,
Shielded from dark clouds,
Unconcerned by the noises of darkness,
Trusting Jesus,
Redemption through His blood,
Harmony,
With the riches of God's grace,
His glorious name,
Warrants praise forever,
May His majestic splendor,
Permeate the whole earth.

Upon the Final Mile-Music

Henry sat where the land gave up its argument with the sea.

The rock beneath him was warm from the day's sun, though evening had started to soften it. Salt filled the air and settled on his lips. Now and then, a wave rolled in with a sound like a deep inhale, then crashed into the dark stones below, sending silver spray into the fading light. The breeze gently pressed against his face, cool and fresh, carrying the sharp scent of salt and seaweed and something ancient he could never quite name. He rested his hands on his knees and listened.

At seventy-two, Henry had learned to love such places—edges, thresholds, the meeting of one thing with another: sea and stone, day and night, memory and hope.

There had been years, of course, when he did not know how to sit still—years of striving, noise, and carrying burdens; regrets, old arguments, harsh words he wished he could take back. Grudges kept secret, as if bitterness could prevent wounds from festering. Ambitions he mistook for purpose. Failures he mistook for identity.

But now, in this late golden hour of his life, he saw more clearly.

"Set aside all broken ways."

The line had returned to him often these past months, not as an accusation but as an invitation. He thought of all the ways grace had met him; sometimes in thunder, sometimes in a whisper, often when he least deserved it. He thought of the patient mercy of God, how Christ had not stood far off demanding cleanliness before welcome, but had come near, healing wounds, His blood cleansing guilt and shame forever.

A stronger wave struck the rocks, and cool droplets kissed his cheek. He smiled. How many times had the Lord lifted him again from among thorns and thistles? How many seasons had seemed barren, only for some stubborn purple flower of faith to rise through the hard ground? He had buried friends, watched his parents leave this world. He had seen plans collapse, and prayers answered in ways he would never have chosen, yet later thanked God for them with tears. Suffering had not been kind, but it had not been empty. Somewhere inside it, often hidden until much later, had been the redemptive thread of God.

"Upon the final mile," he thought silently. He looked toward the horizon, where the sky had become a vast painted canvas—violet, amber, rose, and a red so deep it reminded him of kings and covenants. The clouds, lit from beneath, looked like walls of a mysterious citadel flashing with exquisite colors. For a moment, the whole earth seemed shielded and held, as if darkness itself had been given its boundaries and told, no farther.

He inhaled deeply. The sea's presence filled him with sound, scent, and shifting mist. His bones felt older now, but his soul felt more stable than it ever had in youth. He no longer needed the illusion of infinite time; instead, what he had was better: Assurance.

No assurance in his health, for that was fading in small, undeniable ways. No assurance in his plans, for he had learned how swift plans could scatter like foam.

His assurance was Christ.

Jesus, crucified and risen. Jesus, who had redeemed him through His blood. Jesus, in whom grace was not a fragile feeling but a finished work.

He bowed his head.

"Thank You," he said, and the wind nearly carried the words away.

Thank You for being patient when I was proud.

Thank You for carrying me when I couldn't walk.

Thank You for forgiving what I was afraid to confront.

Thank You for every undeserved mercy.

Thank you that the last phase of life is not a decline into meaninglessness, but a ripening toward home. Another wave came, louder this time, booming in the hollows of the stones, and he felt it in his chest. Yet he was unafraid of the power in it. Something was comforting in the force of the water, in its wild obedience to the One who had drawn the boundaries of the seas. The noises of darkness, the threats that once would have unsettled him—the fear of death, the fear of loss, the fear of becoming small in the eyes of the world—had lost their power.

To choose life, not death; he understood now that this choice was not youthful striving, not frantic self-preservation. It was the daily turning of the heart toward the Lord. It was holiness, not as cold perfection, but as a sacred belonging. It was kneeling before God's grace and rising in gratitude. It was finally learning that the holiest posture could sometimes look like this: an older man seated by the sea, resting in the finished love of Christ, receiving the evening as a gift.

The gulls cried overhead. The waves kept time. The last warmth of the sun touched his face like a blessing.

He thought about the days remaining—not with dread, but with a quiet, almost boyish curiosity. There would still be losses, aches, interruptions, and ordinary sorrows. Yet, there could also be slow breakfasts, unhurried prayer, deeper kindness, wiser silences, long-delayed reconciliations, hymns sung softly in the morning, and Scripture opening like bread in his hands. There might be more beauty to see, more praise to give, and more of God's splendor to notice in the green earth.

He lifted his eyes once more to the reddening sky. A canvas of assurance unfolded. His life had not been a masterpiece of his own making. It had been a rescue, a redemption, a painting still wet with mercy. And now, upon the final mile, he did not need to fear the road ahead. The One who had been faithful in the first mile would be faithful in the last. The sea roared, the rocks stood firm, and the evening deepened around him. He sat there a long while, breathing the salt air, feeling the spray, listening to the waves strike and scatter, and in the secret chambers of his heart there rose a hymn without melody but full of praise. Then, with peace settled deep in him like the tide settling into the shore, he smiled into the wind and waited for the stars.

Ephesians 1:7 (NIV)

In him we have redemption through his blood, the forgiveness of sins, in accordance with the riches of God's grace

PART VII

WHERE DARKNESS FLEES

Torn apart once by betrayal's sting,
Now saved by Christ; redeemed,
Made whole.
Once bitten, twice shy,
This wary heart still feels,
The brewing storm's dark toll.
This detested face from memories,
Returns in a gaze, cold and bare.
Amidst the thunder,
The breeze turns sharp,
And a shadow descends,
Through the air.
A menacing bird,
From the darkened clouds,
Swoops to steal my joy away,
Eager to strike,
Where the scars still seen.
Then my heart begins to pray...
Warfare!
Put on the armor of God.
When the rubber meets,
The road of faith,
Let truth unfold, take courage,
And stand still.
Before the sovereign radiance,
Of God's majestic light,
The darkness flees.

Where Darkness Flees-Music

Clare loved quiet mornings.

In her small apartment on the outskirts of the city, soft light filtered through the kitchen curtains, illuminating the Bible left open beside her coffee cup. Years had passed since she had fled the life that nearly destroyed her. Years since the harsh words, twisting lies, and smiling cruelty that made her doubt the truth of her own soul. In those days, betrayal felt like a blade that never stopped turning.

But Christ had found her there.

Not all at once, not with thunder, but with patient mercy. Through prayers whispered in exhaustion, through tears she could not explain, through the hands of kind women in a small church who asked for nothing and loved her anyway. Piece by piece, Jesus gathered her scattered heart. What had been torn apart, He remade. What had been shamed, He covered. What had nearly died, He called back into life.

Still, healing left her cautious.

Once bitten, twice shy, she sometimes thought, with a sad little smile. She no longer mistook charm for goodness. She no longer feared devotion. Yet even redeemed hearts can tremble when old shadows return.

She saw him on a Friday afternoon.

Clare had gone downtown only to mail a letter and buy bread. The sky had been heavy all day, swollen with rain. She was stepping out of the post office when she lifted her eyes and found him standing across the street.

Her ex-husband.

He had aged, but not softened. His face carried the same cold composure, the same air of injured innocence that once deceived nearly everyone. His gaze found her and held; bare, measuring. Possessive, even now.

At once, the years fell away.

The calm in her chest broke open. Her pulse pounded in her throat. The wind turned sharp as if the weather itself had drawn nearer to hear her fear. Thunder rolled somewhere behind the clouds, and it seemed to her that all the old sorrow had taken wings again—a dark bird dropping from the storm, swooping low to snatch away the hard-won peace God had planted in her.

His mouth moved as if he meant to cross the street—to speak, to charm, to accuse, to manipulate; she did not know. Only the sight of him awakened every scar that had not fully forgotten.

For one terrible instant, Clare felt small.

Then her heart began to pray.

Not aloud, just the desperate inward cry of a woman who knew exactly where her help came from.

Lord Jesus.

That was all.

But it was enough to open heaven in her soul.

A verse rose in her memory, not like something recited, but like a sword placed firmly in her hand: *Put on the whole armor of God to stand against all evil schemes.*

Warfare.

Not the shouting, not the proving, not revenge. This was righteousness. This was the battle to stay in truth when fear demanded surrender.

Clare stood still on the sidewalk with the bread tucked under her arm and the storm gathering overhead. She breathed once, deeply, then again.

Truth: She was not the woman he had defined.

Peace: She no longer belonged to chaos.

Faith: Christ had not brought her this far to abandon her now.

Salvation: Her life was secure with God, beyond his reach.

The Word: No lie survives in the presence of the Living God.

By the time he crossed the street, something had changed, not in him but in her.

He came with that familiar, practiced expression, as if he were the wronged one, as if history were clay in his hands, ready to be shaped into whatever story served him best.

"Clare," he said, with a thin smile. "It's been a long time."

She looked at him fully then, and for the first time in years, she did not feel owned by the memory of his face.

"Yes," she said.

Rain began in slow, cold drops.

He started speaking; fragments of grievance, hints of blame, old hooks dipped in sweetness. He wanted a reaction, the tremor of power he once drew from her pain.

But Clare listened without falling into the trap.

The rubber had met the road of faith.

This was not church language now, not comfort from a pew, not worship while safe among friends. This was the hard test of whether she could stand in the street under a dark sky and remain graceful.

And she did.

When he finished, waiting for her to flinch or argue, Clare answered softly, "I forgive what is behind me, but will not be a doormat ever again. Christ has been too merciful to me for that."

He stared as if he did not understand the language she spoke.

She continued, her voice steady. "You do not define my worth nor decide my peace. My peace is with Jesus Christ."

There was no drama in it, no trembling triumph, only truth, plain and simple.

For a moment, he looked smaller, as if the darkness around him had nowhere left to hide. The old manipulation in his eyes flickered, lost its edge, and with a bitter shrug, he stepped back. The rain came harder then, scattering people along the sidewalks. He muttered something she did not catch and turned away, disappearing into the gray curtain of the storm.

Clare remained where she was.

The thunder still sounded, but farther off now.

She lifted her face into the rain and closed her eyes, not because she was unafraid, but because she discovered something better than fearlessness. She had learned to stand in fear and draw nearer to Christ.

Above the city, the clouds had begun to break. Through their torn edges streamed a serene sovereign light, bright enough to silver the wet pavement and make even the gutters gleam.

Clare knew in that moment, with a certainty deeper than any feeling, that darkness always flees before the sovereign majesty of God.

She walked home in the rain with bread in her arms and gratitude in her heart, as a woman saved.

Once torn by betrayal, now redeemed.

Once hunted by shadows, now sheltered in the radiance of the King.

And beneath the hush of the passing storm, Clare smiled, because Christ had given her more than survival.

He had given her victory.

SCRIPTURE

2 Timothy 1:7 (NIV)

For the Spirit God gave us does not make us timid,
but gives us power, love and self-discipline.

PART VIII

IN THE REALM OF PURE LIGHT

Through the heavy air,
Arrows of grace pierce,
A heart in despair,
Triggering transformation,
Echoes booming loud.
Depths of love,
And life break through the shroud.
Wonders emerged,
Elegance in each sight,
Participant's delight was shining bright.
The courage of conviction,
Looked beyond a stained past,
Gazing towards an angel of light.
The source of light, mystical and pure,
Guides along the path,
Words of perfection.
From the mountain's peak,
A final glance,
The road of trials fades,
No regret in this journey.
Poised for beauty, the everlasting home,
In the grace of light—
Grateful!
Longing no more.

Realm of Pure Light-Music

On the final Friday of his working life, Thomas stayed late after everyone else had gone.

The office, once loud with ringing phones and hurried footsteps, had fallen into a sacred kind of silence. Dust drifted in the slant of evening light like tiny arrows piercing heavy air. On his desk sat a small cardboard box: a Bible, soft at the edges from wear; a framed photograph of his wife and daughter from their youth, a fountain pen, and the brass nameplate he had polished every year without fail.

He placed his hand on the desk one last time.

So many memories lived there— triumphs, failures, quiet prayers whispered before tough meetings, regrets he had carried long, and mercies he never thought he deserved. For a moment, his heart broke as all those years gathered there. The echoes of his life seemed to rise around him—not only the good but also the stained parts: the words he wished he had spoken more kindly, the times he didn't care to listen well, the pride mistaken for strength.

He intuitively opened his Bible to a page and smiled, tears gathering in his eyes. The paper trembled slightly in his hands. Outside, the sinking sun broke through a cloud bank, and the room changed. The grayness lifted. The brass plate shone brightly. The photograph's glass turned golden. Even the box seemed beautiful, as if heaven had leaned close enough to bless ordinary things.

Thomas thought then of all the years ahead: unmapped, quieter, closer to eternity than ambition. Instead of fear, he felt a profound calm. No regret ruled him now.

His life had not been spotless, but it had been held. Beneath every trial, burden, and secret grief, there had been love deeper than failure and brighter than shame; a love that broke through the darkness and called even weary souls into light.

He bowed his head. "Lord," he whispered, "thank You for carrying me farther than I could ever have walked."

The prayer was simple, humble, almost childlike. It seemed to him that all the grander words had fallen away with the years, leaving only what was true: Gratitude, Trust, Longing for home.

When he finally stood to leave, he took one last glance down the long corridor outside his office. It once looked endless. Now it was just a passage, with the evening waiting beyond, tender and bright.

He turned off the light and stepped forward.

And though no angel was visible, Thomas felt as if one was walking beside him in the shimmering dusk, guiding him gently along the path where the road of trials faded behind. He stood before the gates, a glorious light pouring through.

A voice called out to him with love,

"Welcome home, my child."

The world was not ending; It was opening. For the first time in many years, he did not feel the ache of striving. Only peace. Only grace.

Only the shining promise that beyond all labors and goodbyes, there remained a forever home where longing would be no more.

Psalm 36:9 (NIV)

For with you is the fountain of life;
in your light we see light.

PART IX

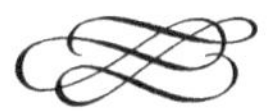

MAJESTIC GRIP

Ground-shaking, life-changing,
A breath held still,
At the window's edge,
Where dawn spills pink across the sky,
And trees bow in silhouette,
To the rising wonder.
A whistling duck struts on the fence,
While a baby squirrel leans in trust,
On the cozy curve of its mother's back.
Truth and Love; entwined.
Spirit to spirit, unbreakable,
Indivisible,
Shining with mysterious,
Ungraspable beauty,
Sacrificial, unchanging, and heavenly!
The finest authorship is born—
Through good, bad,
And the unbearable,
Not ink on paper, but heart on eternity.
A script written in refining flames,
Where no distortion can dwell.
Passion and desire go up in smoke,
Transactional glues evaporate,
And moments of ecstasy move on,
Like the desert sand,
In a storm's aftermath.
Shapeshifting earthly lions,
Shall be humbled,
Or separated,
By the majestic grip,
Of the Gospel Truth.
Short-lived cut flowers end up as trash,
Away from the source,
Of a blossoming life.

Grace flows freely in truth and love,
When forgiven flaws disappear,
Serene worship tunes ascend,
And the soul wells up to pure joy.

Majestic Grip-Music

Glen stood barefoot where the tide kept washing away his footprints and watched the evening paint its colors across the tropical shore. The sea was initially impossibly gentle, blending blue into pink, while the palms leaned inland like worshipers paused in mid-bow. Pelicans glided over the water with solemn purpose. Behind him, a small fence marked the edge of a garden, and on it, a whistling duck perched with absurd dignity, as if to remind the world that tenderness could wear feathers and still speak like a prophet. Near the roots of a sea-grape tree, a tiny squirrel clung to its mother with the quiet confidence of the very young. Everything seemed interconnected by an invisible hand: sky, salt, wind, dependence, praise. Glen once believed Love could survive without Truth, that kindness and peace could prevail without harm, and that avoiding conflict was enough.

Later, in darker years, he swung to the opposite extreme and treated cold precision as a virtue, as if Truth could remain itself when severed from mercy. Living as a divided man, he praised one part of the Gospel while resisting another. Because of this, he wounded those he claimed to care for and allowed himself to be wounded by the false warmth of things that asked nothing holy of him. The waves came in with a hush-like breathing. He thought of the Christian revelation he had tried to outrun: that Truth is not a blade meant to glitter alone, and Love is not a mist that drifts wherever desire blows. In Christ, they belong to each other forever. Truth without Love hardens into cruelty. Love without Truth rots into sentiment, indulgence, and finally lies. Ignoring this is not just an intellectual mistake; it's quietly consenting to the ruin of the soul. A man may call it freedom for a while, dressing it with passion, appetite, and beautiful words. But eventually, the bright flowers cut from their roots begin to smell of death. The sunset deepened, with scarlet clouds burning above the water as if a script was being written and erased at once.

Glen now knew that the best authorship was not the story he told about himself, but the one God carved for him—through good days, bad choices, humiliations, and griefs too heavy to speak aloud. The

Gospel is not meant to flatter his impulses but to discern fire from smoke. It came to expose every bargain mistaken for devotion, every transaction called Love, every passing ecstasy that left him emptier than before. The revelation was profound because it was merciful. It refused to let him keep his distortions and claim they were genuine. A stronger wind swept over the beach, making the palms shiver silver-green beneath the darkening sky.

Then, in that fragile hour between light and darkness, contemplation became prayer. He realized that grace was not permission to remain divided but the power to be made whole. To be forgiven was not to be excused into vagueness but to be gently drawn into the indivisible life of Truth and Love. Into the pierced and radiant heart of Christ. Into a beauty he could only receive, never possess. He lowered his head. The sea continued speaking in long, patient sentences. The duck had flown away, and the little squirrel went hidden among the roots. Above him, the first star appeared—small and unwavering. There, on the beautiful tropical beach, as the last light lingered on the horizon, he understood that every sorrow had sharpened towards this warning and invitation: ignore the union of Truth and Love, and even paradise becomes a mirage; embrace them as one in the Christian revelation, and the soul finally begins to come home.

Isaiah 40:8 (NIV)

The grass withers and the flowers fall,
but the word of our God endures forever.

PART X

THE BANQUET

A celebration of magnitude,
For the bride and the groom.
A sacred covenant of love,
Sharing the ups and downs of life,
Side by side, hand in hand.
To experience the incredible beauty,
Of the celestial showers,
Light raindrops of comfort,
Creating circles from ripples,
Triggering radiating tender love,
Growing steadily, dancing in harmony.
In this good but fallen world,
The hopeful bliss of the divine banquet,
Bears and conquers all pain,
Turning scars into songs.
Joined together in Christ,
To produce good fruits,
To share and bear witness,
Preparing hearts,
For the joyous banquet,
Where burdens become praises,
And every step holds significance.
The straws on the backs are heavy,
The blistering sun penetrates the skin,
A lofty terrain to climb,
Treading by the grace of God,
The weight of the journey softens.
Every mile, every loss,
Leads us deeper into the cross,
Through the dark, through the dawn,
We are held, we are not alone.
Invited to a glorious world yet unseen,
To wear pure linen of righteousness,
With joy and excitement,
Woven not by hands, but by mercy.

The Banquet-Music

On the morning of their wedding, the sky wore a gentle silver veil. It had rained just before dawn—not a storm, but a tender shower, as if heaven itself had stooped low to bless the earth. Drops still clung to the church windows and gathered along the garden stones, forming small circles in every puddle, ripples spreading until they merged, leaving no circle isolated. Helen noticed them as her father led her to the chapel doors, and she thought how love in Christ must be like that: one faithful yes, expanding into countless mercies.

Inside, the groom waited.

Elias stood at the altar with trembling hands and a steady heart. He was not steady because he was unafraid, but because his hope had found a stronger place to rest than his own feelings. Before him stood the wooden cross above the sanctuary, simple and worn. Behind him sat the people who prayed for them, taught them, corrected them, and loved them to this day. And before God, he knew he was about to enter not merely a celebration but a covenant—something weighty and bright, ancient and living.

When Helen stepped into the aisle, he looked at her and felt joy rise inside him like a song. She entered not like someone stepping into a fairy tale, but like a pilgrim entering holy ground with gratitude. White lace wrapped around her like morning light, and although careful hands stitched the dress, it seemed to speak of something deeper, a righteousness not created by human effort but given by mercy. Elias saw tears in her eyes, and they weren't tears of fear. They were tears born from wonder. They stood side by side, hand in hand.

The Priest spoke of covenant, of Christ and His Church, of love that is not just a feeling but a sacred promise. He spoke of a good yet fallen world where joy is real, and grief is real too; where shoulders tire, and the sun can blister the skin along the steep terrain of life. He did not hide from them that there would be losses, misunderstandings, sickness, waiting, repentance, and sorrow. Yet neither did he speak as one without hope.

For this was a Christian wedding.

And Christian hope is never fragile.

It dares to face pain head-on and declare that pain will not have the final say. It believes that in Christ, scars can transform into songs. It trusts that every mile, every burden carried together, leads deeper into the mystery of the cross; and, therefore, deeper into lasting love. The covenant they entered that day was not built on the fragile strength of two human hearts but on the pierced and risen heart of Jesus.

When they exchanged their vows, the chapel grew very still. Elias promised not only to cherish Helen during times of laughter but also to stand beside her through darkness and dawn. Helen promised more than tenderness; she pledged faithfulness during hardships. They offered each other not a life free of wounds but one that would testify to a Savior who redeems them. Their love would not be an escape from the world's sorrow but a lantern within it.

And that was part of their joy. For they knew marriage was never meant to end in itself. It was a signpost, a table set in advance, a foretaste of the divine banquet still to come. Joined together in Christ, they longed to bear good fruit—to welcome the weary, to strengthen the fainthearted, and to prepare hearts for the greater banquet where burdens become praises. Even their ordinary days, they believed, would carry eternal significance: shared prayers in the kitchen, forgiveness before sleep, bread broken at the table, hands clasped in hospital rooms, hymns sung through grief, children perhaps, guests certainly, and a thousand hidden acts of grace known fully only to God.

When the rings were placed on their fingers, they felt both small and glorious; small because they were just bands of gold, glorious because they pointed to something eternal. A circle without a break. A promise without retreating.

Then came the pronouncement.

And when at last they turned to walk back down the aisle together, husband and wife, the rain began again outside—gentle, luminous, almost musical against the chapel roof. The guests smiled and laughed, lifting flowers and faces toward the sound. Helen leaned closer to Elias, and he squeezed her hand. They stepped into that silver morning not as two dreamers expecting an easy path, but as two saints filled with great eternal hope.

Ahead of them lay miles they could not yet see. There would be heavy straws on bent backs, steep climbs beneath a hot sun, losses that hollowed them out, and nights that seemed too long. But grace would meet them there. And the weight of the journey, carried with Christ, would soften. Through every valley and every dawn, they would be held. They would not be alone.

Beyond every earthly joy and sorrow, the unseen realm shone brightly; a glorious world not yet visible but already promised. All their love, repentance, devotion, laughter, and endurance would someday be gathered into that glorious feast. So they moved forward with joy and excitement, clothed in mercy, hand in hand. And heaven, it seemed, was closer than the rain.

REVELATION 19:9 (NIV)

Then the angel said to me, “Write this: Blessed are those who are invited to the wedding supper of the Lamb!” And he added, “These are the true words of God.”

PART XI

THE RESCUE

From facade and fragile charade,
A gateway to the ultimate truth,
The ever-loving sacred heart of Christ,
Pursuing us with love and perfection.
Embracing love in truth,
Keeping munitions,
From dangerous wolves,
By humble Spirit-guided discernment,
Learning the living word of God.
The joy of freedom,
Not born of misguided compassion,
That shields destructive paths,
And validates masked deceptions.
To carry the message of redemption,
Through toxic air,
Aiding loving hearts,
To breathe and flourish.
Belonging as branches in the true vine,
Drawn from the temporal,
Into the eternal.
From the tangled web,
Of luminous delusions,
To meaningless excesses,
Setting aside the needs of many,
Sowing fields of chaos and despair.
Not every voice that sounds so sweet,
Can heal the soul or make us free,
Living and growing in the true vine,
You are the truth that sets us free.
With the breath of life infused,
Acting on worthy causes,
With humility and firmness,
To endure a journey of abiding faith.

The Rescue-Music

He had learned, over the years, how easy it was to be ignored in a church foyer. Steve was the kind of man people passed by with polite smiles and unfulfilled promises. He stacked chairs after Bible study, wiped coffee rings from folding tables, and listened more than he spoke. He was not loud, not fashionable, nor skilled in the gentle language that makes difficult things seem easy. His faith was simple, stern, and tender all at once, like hands calloused from labor but lifted gently in prayer. For a long time, he quietly endured the ache.

He sat through conversations where fellow Christians equated surrender with kindness and called moral compromise compassion. He witnessed sin renamed as self-expression, repentance overlooked, and the sharp mercy of truth dulled into something marginal. Time and again, he saw those who claimed Christ speak as if love meant blessing every desire and leaving every chain unbroken.

The grief of it pressed into him more deeply than anger. It was not disgust that troubled him, but sorrow. Sorrow for souls. Sorrow for the young. Sorrow for the weary and confused who came looking for bread and were handed mist.

One evening, after a gathering where laughter had floated easily around topics he believed should have brought tears, Steve walked home beneath a bruised purple sky. The wind was cold, and the city air felt heavy, as if even breathing required endurance. He entered his small apartment, placed his worn Bible on the table, and fell to his knees.

"Lord," he whispered, "keep me from pride. Keep me from bitterness. But do not let me call darkness light." Silence responded first.

Then came the familiar steadiness he had experienced in long suffering: not thunder, not spectacle, but the quiet weight of conviction. He rose, lit a lamp, and began to write. The poem came like a wound opening for healing, each line carved out of prayer and fire: From facade and fragile charade, a gateway to the ultimate truth, the ever-loving sacred heart of Christ, pursuing us with love and perfection. He wrote not to impress, but to testify. Not to wound, but to warn. His pen moved with the force of a man who feared God more than rejection.

"Embracing love in truth,
Keeping munitions,
From dangerous wolves,
By humble Spirit-guided discernment,
Learning the living word of God."

When he finished, dawn was beginning to silver the edges of the window. Steve read the poem aloud, and his own voice trembled. In it was his protest against counterfeit mercy, against the luminous delusions that sparkled like holiness while hollowing out the soul. But there was more than protest. There was hope. There was Christ.

The next Sunday, he did what few expected of him. When the discussion again turned toward affirming what Scripture warned against, and the room filled with nods, careful phrases, and sentimental evasions, Steve stood. At first, no one paid much attention. He was just Steve—quiet, unassuming Steve. But then he began to read. His voice was unpolished, yet it carried, with the rough strength of a bell rung in bad weather.

"The joy of freedom,
Not born of misguided compassion,
That shields destructive paths,
And validates masked deceptions."

The room fell silent. Some faces hardened, others lowered, and a few looked stricken, as if something long buried had been unearthed. Steve continued reading, not with rage, but with tears bright in his eyes.

"To carry the message of redemption,
Through toxic air,
Aiding loving hearts to breathe and flourish,
Belonging as branches in the true vine,
Drawn from the temporal into the eternal."

He spoke of Christ's love as sacred, one that did not flatter sinners but called them out of death. He explained that compassion without truth was not compassion at all—just abandonment with a smile. He declared that the Church was not made to mirror the age but to witness against it with grace and courage. His hands trembled, but he refused to sit down.

Then came the closing lines, and they seemed to hit harder than all the rest:

"Not every voice that sounds so sweet,
Can heal the soul or make us free.
Living and growing in the true vine,
You are the truth that sets us free."

For several moments after he finished, no one spoke.

Steve knew what it cost him. He knew some would call him harsh, rigid, unloving. He understood he would leave that room more disregarded by some than ever before. But beneath the pain, there was peace—deep, clear, unshakable peace. He had not spoken to seek approval. He spoke because silence had become a kind of betrayal.

And in the stillness, an older woman in the back started to weep.

Then a young man, restless, guarded, burdened by private confusion, asked in a broken voice, "But what if I want that freedom? What if I'm tired of pretending?"

Steve turned toward him, and all the sternness on his face softened into compassion made pure by truth.

"Then Christ is still calling," he said. "Not to condemn you without hope, but to redeem you completely."

That morning, the room did not split as cleanly as people expected. Conviction had entered, and so had mercy. Not the shallow mercy of indulgence, but the costly mercy that leads sinners to the cross and teaches them to live.

Steve walked home later beneath the same open sky, still a disregarded man in the world's eyes, perhaps in the Church's eyes too. Yet his heart was strangely light.

For he knew that faithfulness is not measured by applause, and that a lonely voice, yielded to God, can become a trumpet in an age of fog.

And though many would forget his name, the truth he had spoken would remain; like a flame kept alive in bitter wind, refusing to bow, refusing to die.

John 14:6 (NIV)

Jesus answered, "I am the way and the truth and the life.
No one comes to the Father except through me."

PART XII

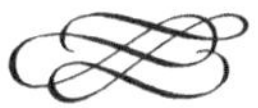

VICTORIOUS

Along the stream beside a campfire,
Glowing embers keep the air warm,
Leaves and twigs moved,
Through flowing waters,
The full moon adorning the clear skies.
On a dazzling night of shining stars,
Creation sings God's glory,
Evoking amazing scriptural visions,
Of a flaming torch,
And a smoking firepot,
God's unconditional covenant,
With Abraham,
And the burning coal,
That touched Isaiah,
Removing guilt,
And the forgiveness of sins.
The Holy week, feeling the gravity,
Drawing near.
We deeply revere,
God's unfathomable love,
Covenant faithfulness,
The ultimate eternal fulfillment,
Through the sacrifice,
Of our Lord and Savior Jesus Christ.
We worship,
Glory to God in the highest,
Celebrate the resurrection.
The victory of God's love,
In Christ's sacrifice,
Poured out for our peace,
To live without fear, in love and joy,
By His presence in the midst,
In this fallen world,
With unerring guidance,
Of the Holy Spirit.

Victorious-Music

By the time the sun dipped behind the pines, the small camp by the stream had become its own little world. Hannah knelt by the fire, feeding it thin branches one at a time. The embers glowed softly, spreading warmth into the cool night air. Next to her, the stream flowed steadily over rocks, carrying leaves and twigs into the distance, shimmering in silver. Above all, the full moon hung like a lamp in the clear sky, and the stars shone so brightly that it felt as if heaven had drawn close enough to touch.

Her grandfather sat across from her, wrapped in an old wool blanket, his Bible resting closed in his lap. He did not speak for a long time. He simply watched the flames as if they were telling an ancient story.

"It feels holy tonight," Hannah whispered at last. Her grandfather smiled. "Creation has a way of remembering." The words settled over her heart. She listened: the stream singing over rock, the crackle of fire, the wind stirring the branches. Everything seemed alive with praise. Not loud praise, but deep praise—the kind that filled the spaces between breaths.

Her eyes stayed fixed on the flames. "Do you think Abraham saw a fire like this?" Her grandfather looked into the blaze. "Maybe brighter. Maybe fiercer. But yes, I think the night he waited on God, and the smoking firepot and flaming torch passed through the darkness, it might have looked something like this. A sign that God binds Himself in love and never breaks His word." Hannah pulled her knees up and watched a spark rise. She imagined Abraham under a sky like this one, waiting, wondering, trusting. Then another thought crossed her mind. "And Isaiah?" Her grandfather nodded slowly. "A burning coal to cleanse his lips. Mercy that came like fire, not to destroy, but to make holy."

Hannah fell quiet again. Holy Week was only days away, and lately its weight had been pressing on her heart. She had tried to explain it to her friends once—why sorrow and joy seemed to walk together in these sacred days—but the words had failed her. Tonight, though, sitting beside the stream and fire beneath the moon's white glow, she began to feel the truth of it more clearly.

The same God who made a covenant with Abraham, the same God who purified Isaiah, had given more than a sign, more than a coal, more than a promise spoken from afar. He had given His Son.

The thought came not like thunder but like light spreading over still water.

Jesus Christ—offered in love, poured out for peace, bearing guilt, defeating sin, opening the way where fear had once stood guard. The cross was terrible, yes, but it was not the end of the story. It had become, by God's own mysterious glory, the doorway to life. And beyond the passion of Friday waited the brightness of resurrection morning.

Her grandfather opened the Bible and read softly, his voice almost blending with the stream. The words spoke of sacrifice, love stronger than death, and a tomb emptied by glory. Hannah closed her eyes and listened, and it seemed to her that the whole night listened too—the trees, the stars, the flowing water, the breathing earth. When he finished, neither of them spoke.

The fire burned low, but its warmth persisted. Somewhere in the dark woods, an owl called once and then fell silent. Hannah lifted her face to the sky. She no longer felt small in the frightening way she sometimes did. Instead, she felt supported. The world was still broken, still hurting, still waiting—but God had not abandoned it. His love had entered, and His presence remained in the midst of it. His Spirit still guided, steady and unseen as the current beside her. The victory had already been won.

Not by swords, nor by kings, nor by the strength of men—but by love that would not fail, by mercy that endured, by Christ risen and reigning. The stars above her no longer seemed distant but like witnesses. The stream no longer merely flowed; it rejoiced. Even the fire, with its glowing embers, seemed to testify.

Creation sings God's glory, she thought.

So there, beside the campfire and the stream, under the full moon and the dazzling array of stars, Hannah bowed her head and gave thanks to God in the highest: for covenant faithfulness, for forgiveness, for the cross, for the empty tomb, for peace that casts out fear, and for joy that no darkness can overcome.

The night remained quiet.

But it was the quiet of something triumphant.

The quiet of a world made beautiful by hope.

The quiet of a soul that knew, at last, what it meant to be victorious.

Psalm 19:1-2 (NIV)

The heavens declare the glory of God;
the skies proclaim the work of his hands.
Day after day they pour forth speech;
night after night they reveal knowledge.

www.ingramcontent.com/pod-product-compliance
Lightning Source LLC
LaVergne TN
LVHW010951110826
845149LV00015B/3295

9798995964810